Big Cats

Published by Wildlife Education, Ltd.
12233 Thatcher Court, Poway, California 92064
contact us at: 1-800-477-5034
e-mail us at: animals@zoobooks.com
visit us at: www.zoobooks.com

ISBN 1-888153-38-5

Big Cats

Created and Written by
John Bonnett Wexo

Scientific Consultant
Edward J. Maruska
Director
Cincinnati Zoological Gardens

Contents

MOUNTAIN LION
Felis concolor

JAGUAR
Panthera onca

Big cats are among the most beautiful creatures on earth. Their strength and grace, combined with their often secretive natures, have fascinated people for ages.

The major difference between most big cats and the little cats is that big cats roar but cannot purr. Mountain lions, snow leopards, clouded leopards, and cheetahs cannot roar. Of these, snow leopards and cheetahs are

AFRICAN LIONS
Panthera leo

LEOPARDS, SPOTTED AND DARK PHASES
Panthera pardus

SNOW LEOPARD
Panthera Uncia

CLOUDED LEOPARD
Neofelis nebulosa

CHEETAH
Acinonyx jubatus

SIBERIAN TIGER
Panthera tigris

considered big cats. Other big cats are the leopard, the lion, the tiger, and the jaguar. The clouded leopard is considered a bridge between big cats and little cats and has some characteristics of both groups.

As a group, big cats have a broad range. They are found north of the Arctic Circle, in steaming tropical jungles, and on open plains. Every continent but Europe, Australia, and Antarctica has its big cats.

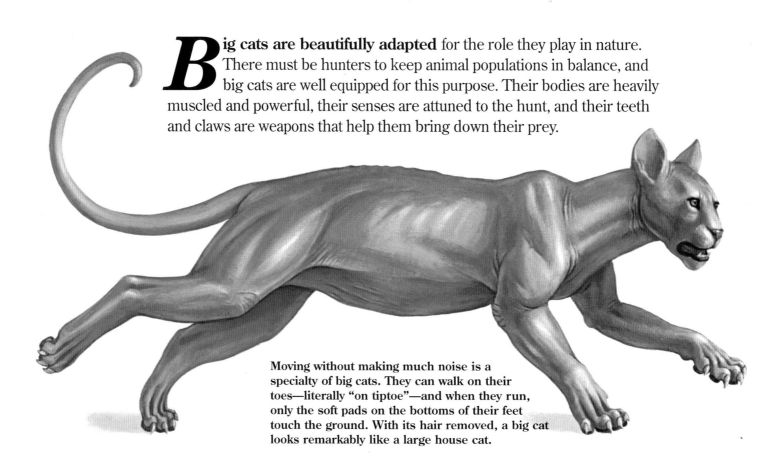

Big cats are beautifully adapted for the role they play in nature. There must be hunters to keep animal populations in balance, and big cats are well equipped for this purpose. Their bodies are heavily muscled and powerful, their senses are attuned to the hunt, and their teeth and claws are weapons that help them bring down their prey.

Moving without making much noise is a specialty of big cats. They can walk on their toes—literally "on tiptoe"—and when they run, only the soft pads on the bottoms of their feet touch the ground. With its hair removed, a big cat looks remarkably like a large house cat.

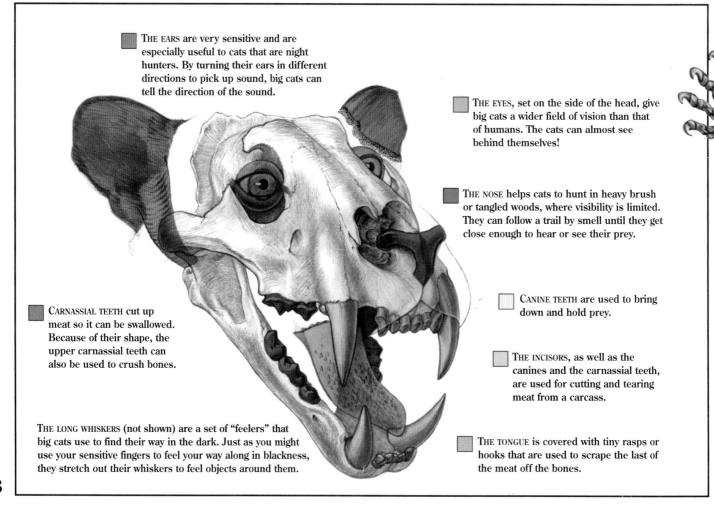

THE EARS are very sensitive and are especially useful to cats that are night hunters. By turning their ears in different directions to pick up sound, big cats can tell the direction of the sound.

THE EYES, set on the side of the head, give big cats a wider field of vision than that of humans. The cats can almost see behind themselves!

THE NOSE helps cats to hunt in heavy brush or tangled woods, where visibility is limited. They can follow a trail by smell until they get close enough to hear or see their prey.

CANINE TEETH are used to bring down and hold prey.

CARNASSIAL TEETH cut up meat so it can be swallowed. Because of their shape, the upper carnassial teeth can also be used to crush bones.

THE INCISORS, as well as the canines and the carnassial teeth, are used for cutting and tearing meat from a carcass.

THE LONG WHISKERS (not shown) are a set of "feelers" that big cats use to find their way in the dark. Just as you might use your sensitive fingers to feel your way along in blackness, they stretch out their whiskers to feel objects around them.

THE TONGUE is covered with tiny rasps or hooks that are used to scrape the last of the meat off the bones.

Big cats are incredibly strong. Powerful muscles in both the front and rear legs provide great driving force for running and jumping. Tigers are like battering rams, able to knock down animals weighing more than twice as much as they do.

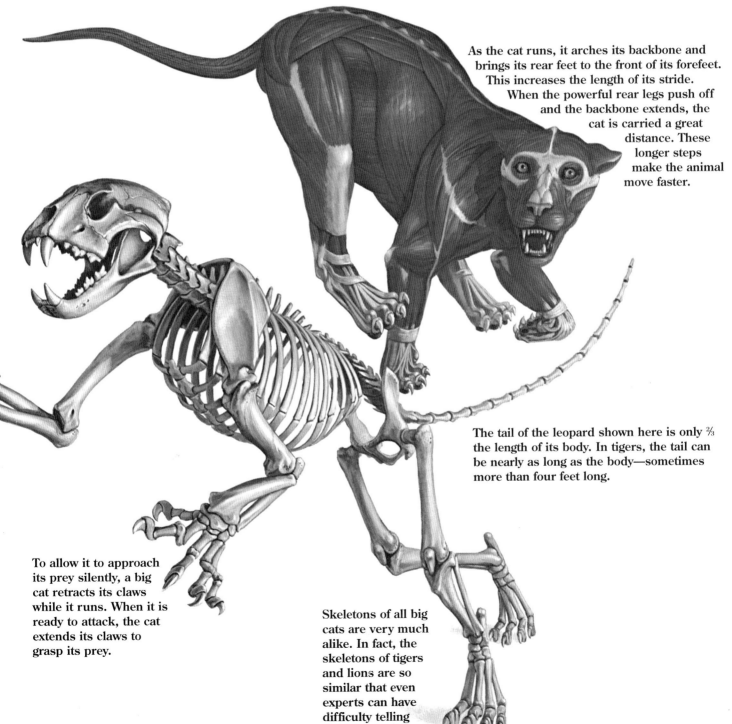

As the cat runs, it arches its backbone and brings its rear feet to the front of its forefeet. This increases the length of its stride. When the powerful rear legs push off and the backbone extends, the cat is carried a great distance. These longer steps make the animal move faster.

The tail of the leopard shown here is only ⅔ the length of its body. In tigers, the tail can be nearly as long as the body—sometimes more than four feet long.

To allow it to approach its prey silently, a big cat retracts its claws while it runs. When it is ready to attack, the cat extends its claws to grasp its prey.

Skeletons of all big cats are very much alike. In fact, the skeletons of tigers and lions are so similar that even experts can have difficulty telling them apart.

Leopards and jaguars are often confused because of the similar pattern of their spots. This is not the only similarity between them. Both are equally at home in a wide variety of settings—swamps, forests, mountains, and grasslands. Both can survive on a wide variety of different food items, from large herd animals to insects. And both have maintained large ranges despite the destructive activities of people.

The key to the success of both the jaguar and the leopard has been the ability of these animals to adapt to changing conditions.

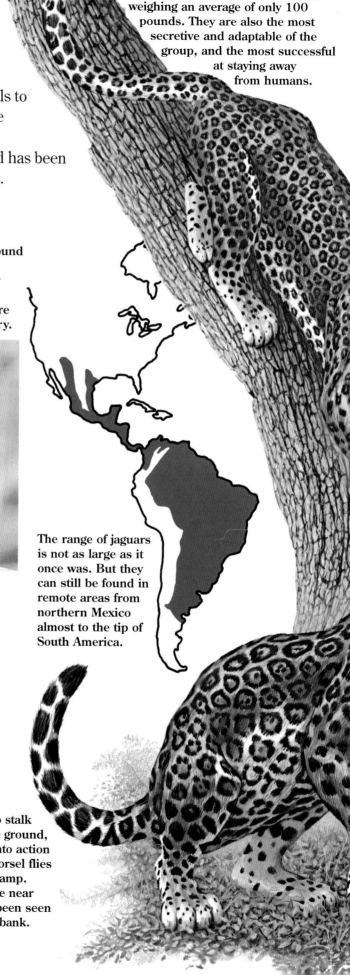

Leopards are the smallest of the big cats, weighing an average of only 100 pounds. They are also the most secretive and adaptable of the group, and the most successful at staying away from humans.

Dark leopards and jaguars are found most often in deep forests and jungles. It seems likely that their coat color helps them to hide in shadows. Cats of lighter colors are more apt to occur in open country.

Both jaguars and leopards may be born with dark, nearly black coats. A close look in the right light shows spots hidden in the dark coat.

The range of jaguars is not as large as it once was. But they can still be found in remote areas from northern Mexico almost to the tip of South America.

Jaguars prefer to stalk their prey on the ground, but will spring into action even if a tasty morsel flies into a muddy swamp. Jaguars like to be near water and have been seen fishing from the bank.

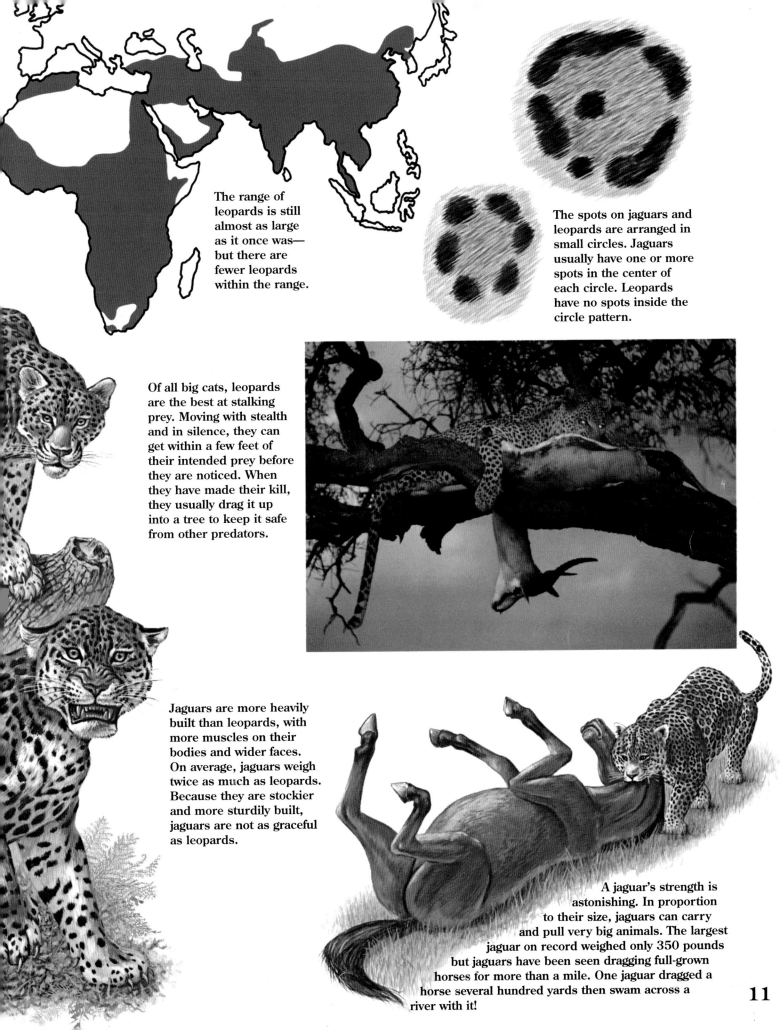

The range of leopards is still almost as large as it once was—but there are fewer leopards within the range.

The spots on jaguars and leopards are arranged in small circles. Jaguars usually have one or more spots in the center of each circle. Leopards have no spots inside the circle pattern.

Of all big cats, leopards are the best at stalking prey. Moving with stealth and in silence, they can get within a few feet of their intended prey before they are noticed. When they have made their kill, they usually drag it up into a tree to keep it safe from other predators.

Jaguars are more heavily built than leopards, with more muscles on their bodies and wider faces. On average, jaguars weigh twice as much as leopards. Because they are stockier and more sturdily built, jaguars are not as graceful as leopards.

A jaguar's strength is astonishing. In proportion to their size, jaguars can carry and pull very big animals. The largest jaguar on record weighed only 350 pounds but jaguars have been seen dragging full-grown horses for more than a mile. One jaguar dragged a horse several hundred yards then swam across a river with it!

11

These lion cubs look ready to cuddle and spend most of their time playing.

*L*ions are different from the other big cats in several important ways. All of the others are solitary—they live alone most of the time and usually hunt alone as well. But lions live in groups called prides that can include as many as 35 lions, although a large pride is often broken into smaller groups within the pride.

Unlike other big cats, adult lions do not have stripes or spots on their coats. While tigers, leopards, and jaguars often live in forests and swamps, African lions prefer the wide-open spaces. It could be that life on the open plains has forced the lion to adopt a different method of living and hunting that requires cooperation.

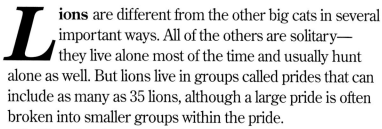

When lions have just eaten, they become lazy. Animals that would normally be prey for the lion are ignored. These zebras know they don't need to run away, but they watch the lions for any sudden moves.

Only male lions have manes, which can vary in color from tawny gold to reddish brown to black.

A lion's roar can carry for more than five miles.

Lions spend most of the day sleeping or lying in the shade relaxing. It has been said that the lion is the laziest animal in Africa.

Lion cubs are born in litters of four or less, as a rule. When young, their coats are spotted. As they grow older, the spots disappear.

In the past, lions had a much larger range. Less than 2,000 years ago, there were lions in southeastern Europe. Today, lions are limited to parts of Africa and a very small game preserve in India's Gir Forest.

PRESENT RANGE
FORMER RANGE

Asian lions look very much like African lions. It was once thought that Asian lions had shorter manes, but this is not true. Both types may have either long or short manes.

Old males are usually driven out of the pride to be replaced by younger adult males. Unable to hunt fast-moving prey, the banished old males may start hunting people.

The lions in a pride seem to get along well—except at mealtimes. The social order says that males eat their fill first. Then females and young move in. There can be fights over a favorite piece of meat, and even cubs will defend their parts of the kill against adults. Adult lions can eat as much as 40 pounds of meat at a single sitting. If the kill was small, the cubs may lose out.

At an early age, lion cubs practice to become hunters by stalking beetles, butterflies, sticks, stones, and each other.

Lions are the only big cats that usually hunt in groups. They surround the prey and drive it into a trap, as shown at right. Females do most of the hunting, and males take a part of the kill from the females after the hunt is over. When the prey is large, the males may join in the hunt to add their strength. Group hunting is very effective. A single lion hunting is only successful 17 percent of the time, or less. The success rate nearly doubles with group hunting.

LIONS CIRCLE AROUND PREY

LIONS CIRCLE AROUND PREY

LIONS CIRCLE AROUND PREY

LIONS SHOW THEM-SELVES TO SCARE PREY

PREY STAMPEDES

HIDING LIONS WAIT FOR PREY

15

Tigers are often called the most beautiful of the big cats, as well as the most powerful and most dangerous to man. Their reputation for beauty and power is well deserved. There can be few things as elegant as a tiger's striped coat, and they are the most muscular and the largest of the big cats. But the threat they pose to man has been greatly exaggerated.

No two tigers have the same pattern of stripes. Face markings are so distinctive that they can be used to tell one tiger from another.

If tigers had no stripes, they might starve to death. Because they are not fast runners, they must get close to their prey in order to catch it. Their stripes help them to blend in with the tall grass and allow them to get close to their prey. Even then, tigers are only successful in the hunt 1 out of every 10 or 20 times.

Tigers have the largest canine teeth of any meat-eating land animal. But even the tooth of a very large tiger looks small next to the eight-inch tooth of a gigantic and extinct saber-toothed tiger.

When the weather gets warm, tigers often can be found in a cool pool of water. Unlike most cats, tigers love the water and swim well.

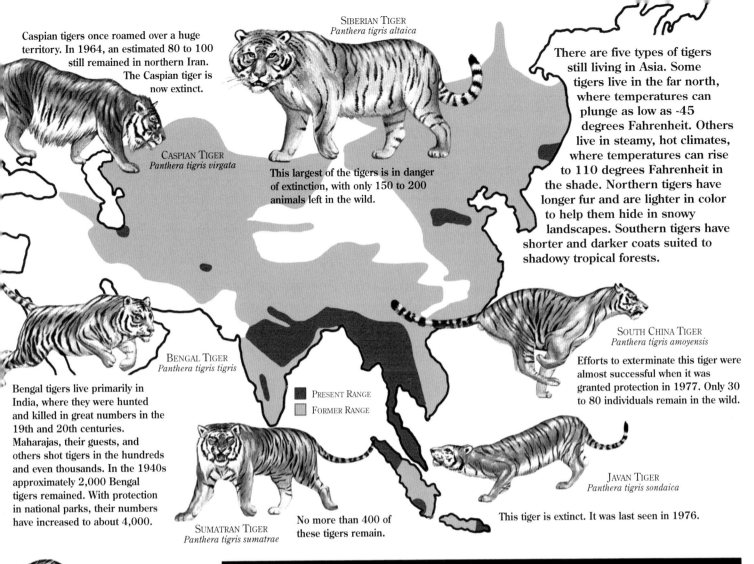

Caspian tigers once roamed over a huge territory. In 1964, an estimated 80 to 100 still remained in northern Iran. The Caspian tiger is now extinct.

CASPIAN TIGER
Panthera tigris virgata

SIBERIAN TIGER
Panthera tigris altaica

This largest of the tigers is in danger of extinction, with only 150 to 200 animals left in the wild.

There are five types of tigers still living in Asia. Some tigers live in the far north, where temperatures can plunge as low as -45 degrees Fahrenheit. Others live in steamy, hot climates, where temperatures can rise to 110 degrees Fahrenheit in the shade. Northern tigers have longer fur and are lighter in color to help them hide in snowy landscapes. Southern tigers have shorter and darker coats suited to shadowy tropical forests.

BENGAL TIGER
Panthera tigris tigris

■ PRESENT RANGE
■ FORMER RANGE

SOUTH CHINA TIGER
Panthera tigris amoyensis

Efforts to exterminate this tiger were almost successful when it was granted protection in 1977. Only 30 to 80 individuals remain in the wild.

Bengal tigers live primarily in India, where they were hunted and killed in great numbers in the 19th and 20th centuries. Maharajas, their guests, and others shot tigers in the hundreds and even thousands. In the 1940s approximately 2,000 Bengal tigers remained. With protection in national parks, their numbers have increased to about 4,000.

SUMATRAN TIGER
Panthera tigris sumatrae

No more than 400 of these tigers remain.

JAVAN TIGER
Panthera tigris sondaica

This tiger is extinct. It was last seen in 1976.

INDOCHINESE TIGER
Panthera tigris corbetti

There are 1,050 to 1,750 of these tigers spread across Southeast Asia.

This gathering of tigers is unusual. As a rule, tigers hunt alone and don't like to share their kills with others. These tigers may be young members of the same family that have not yet gone out on their own. When fully grown, a tiger needs about 15 pounds of food every day to survive.

P**eople have loved and feared** big cats throughout history. Ancient tribes worshiped them. The Egyptians, who were probably the first to domesticate small cats, mummified them (as shown at left) and kept big cats in zoos as symbols of royal power. Nations have placed pictures of them on flags, and kings and emperors have worn their skins as part of their royal regalia. To this day, in the minds of most people, big cats stand for courage and majesty.

For centuries, the cheetah was known as "the hunting leopard," and was used by man to help bring down game. Running at speeds exceeding 60 miles per hour, this fastest of all land animals caught the prey and held it until the human hunters arrived. The emperor Kublai Khan was said to have owned 1,000 hunting cheetahs.

Big cats are in danger throughout the world, although most of them are protected by law. Illegal hunting, or poaching, is on the increase. Spotted fur coats are still sought after in many parts of the world, as this game warden demonstrates with a stack of illegal skins. More recently, big cats—notably tigers—have been killed for their bones and other body parts. These are in great demand in Asia, where they bring large sums of money for their supposed medicinal value.

To the ancient peoples of South America, the strength and beauty of the jaguar qualified it as one of the highest gods. This handsome pot from the Moche culture of coastal Peru shows a jaguar holding a dog.

The lion was a favorite animal of the ancient Assyrians and Babylonians. As a result, when these two civilizations began the study of astronomy, they named one of the most important groups of stars after the lion.

Great prestige was once the reward for killing a tiger. To please high-ranking hunters, a special tape measure, with only 11 inches to the foot, was used to measure their trophies. Many a 10-foot tiger suddenly became an 11-foot tiger. In 1965, one Maharaja reported that his total take of tigers was *only* 1,150.

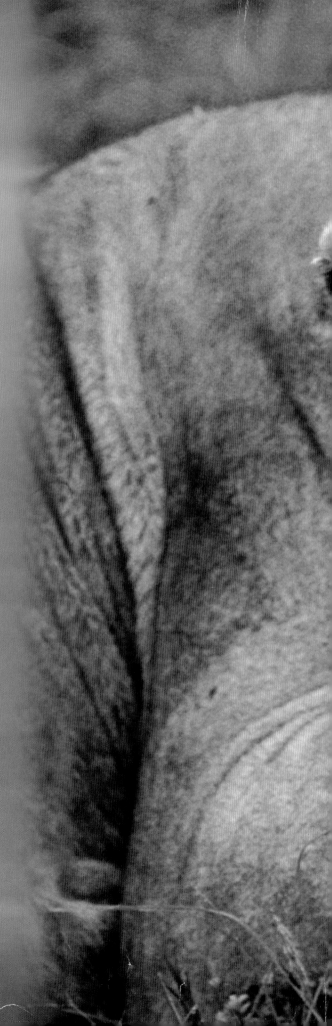

All big cats are offered some protection, which is often ignored. Most are endangered or vulnerable to extinction. Except for the Masai lion of East Africa, all other lion subspecies are endangered. Two are extinct.

One hundred years ago, lions could be found throughout Africa and over much of Asia. Today, the Barbary lion is gone from northern Africa and the Cape lion is extinct in South Africa. The Senegal lion from West Africa and the Angolan lion of southern Africa are both endangered, as is the Transvaal lion, which lives only in Kruger National Park. The once-widespread Asian lion is reduced to about 250 individuals in a small preserve in India.

Although prized by the fur trade for its coat, the solitary cheetah is mostly threatened by loss of habitat and the resulting competition for food with larger, stronger predators. When a cheetah makes a kill, a larger predator often steals it. There are about 20,000 cheetahs left in Africa.

All leopards are endangered except for the African leopard that lives below the Sahara. Although its numbers dwindle, this leopard's wide range and ability to avoid humans may help it to survive. In the early 1990s, an Austrian hunter paid $16,000 to kill a snow leopard. Poaching of snow leopards and other wildlife continues to grow throughout central Asia.

The most rapidly disappearing big cat is the tiger. Aside from habitat loss, the tiger's biggest threat is from poaching. Laws made to protect these endangered animals are being ignored to satisfy the large, lucrative, and ever-escalating black-market trade in tiger parts. Internationally, the traffic in illegal wildlife is second only to drug smuggling. The Caspian, Java and Bali tigers all became extinct in the last half of the 20th century. At the current rate of slaughter, the rest of the world's tigers will soon follow them. India is home to 2/3 of the world's tigers, with a population of about 4,000.

Poachers kill tigers in India, Indonesia, China, and Russia. If the illegal traffic in tigers is not stopped, it is likely that other big cats from Africa and elsewhere will find their way into the markets of Asia.

Index